The Relationship between Religion & Politics in Islam

by

Hazrat Mirza Tahir Ahmad[rta]

ISLAM INTERNATIONAL PUBLICATIONS LTD.

The Relationship between Religion & Politics in Islam

A speech delivered by
Hazrat Mirza Tahir Ahmad, Khalifatul-Masih IV[rta],
at the Inter-Religious Consults, Suriname,
on 3rd June 1991

First published in the UK, 1992 (1 85372 478 5)
Present editon published in the UK & India, 2017

© Islam International Publications Ltd.

Published by
Islam International Publications Ltd.
(Additional Wakalat-e-Tasneef)
Islamabad, Sheephatch Lane
Tilford, Surrey GU10 2AQ, UK

For further information please visit www.alislam.org.

ISBN 978-1-84880-889-8

CONTENTS

ABOUT THE AUTHOR

Hazrat Mirza Tahir Ahmad[rta] was the spiritual head of the international Ahmadiyya Muslim Community from June 1982–April 2003. He was the fourth Khalifah (successor) of Hazrat Mirza Ghulam Ahmad[as] who proclaimed to be the Messiah and Reformer of the Latter Days, promised by all the great religions of the world. His community is a dynamic, worldwide, missionary force in Islam.

Hazrat Mirza Tahir Ahmad[rta] was born on 18 December 1928 in Qadian, India. He was educated in India, Pakistan and the UK—at The London School of Oriental and African Studies. In 1982 he was elected as the head of the worldwide Ahmadiyya Muslim Community following the demise of the Third Khalifah[rta].

Hazrat Mirza Tahir Ahmad[rta] travelled extensively and often delivered addresses to audiences including people from all walks of life and vastly different cultures. His addresses and other meetings were often accompanied by question and answer sessions. He was always ready to respond to questions agitating the minds of his audience on any topic, religious or temporal. Whatever the nature of the questions, he seemed to handle them comfortably in the light of his deep understanding of religion, which pervaded his thinking.

He had written many books in Urdu as well as some in English. *Murder in the Name of Allah; Islam's Response to Contemporary Issues; Absolute Justice, Kindness and Kinship—The Three Creative Principles;* and *Revelation, Rationality, Knowledge and Truth,* are some of his English publications which the reader may find of interest.

FOREWORD

In today's world, Shariah law frequently takes the forefront of international headlines as a symbol of Islamic oppression and terrorism. The sensitivities surrounding this issue have divided populations with a polarizing effect. Some Western nations and states have even gone to the extent of passing legislation against Shariah law. However, the fact of the matter is that these extremes are fueled by fear and misunderstanding, much of which Muslims are directly responsible for.

In his speech addressing IRIS (Inter-Religious Council in Suriname) entitled *The Relationship between Religion & Politics in Islam*, Hazrat Mirza Tahir Ahmad[rta] analyzes the complexities of implementing Shariah law from various angles. His assessment is refreshingly accommodating to modern structures of governance in pluralistic societies. Nevertheless, he bases all of his conclusions directly from the Holy Quran, Hadith and Sunnah.

He also calls out the hypocrisy so rampantly witnessed in Muslim countries. He rightfully admonishes Muslims to first reform themselves before oppressively imposing their interpretation of Shariah law upon others. He indicates that the combination of these factors have resulted in conditions that make Shariah law impractical, oppressive and against the very spirit it was designed to promote.

We are grateful to Naseer-ud-Din Shams and Naser-ud-Din Shams for their valuable assistance in bringing this manuscript to publication. May Allah the Almighty reward them abundantly. *Aameen.*

Munir-ud-Din Shams
Additional Wakilut-Tasneef,
January, 2017, London

*The Relationship between
Religion & Politics in Islam*

OPENING REMARKS

by the Chairperson of IRIS

It is for me a privilege to welcome you on behalf of IRIS and the community here to this meeting. IRIS stands for 'Interreligieuze Raad Suriname' or 'Inter-Religious Council In Suriname'.

Welcome to our meeting. You are here for a week and as you have already felt and experienced, you are most welcome here in Suriname, which is called the country of hospitality and laughter.

We have read already something about your person, your education and your formation. Also about your mission: to Suriname and mission to the world. And, as we could understand, your mission is mainly to bring people together. People of several races, various countries and various cultures. And your message is a message of respect of one another, respectful thinking, acceptance and understanding; to bring justice and peace among people.

It is in this context that we invited you this evening to be with us here—with IRIS in this community—to share with you, our views, our insights and our ideas on this topic. IRIS is a group of religious leaders in Suriname and it exists for about two or three years. But up till now, we have only focused on working together, instead of dialogue together. Working together for the well-being of the Suriname people. And, in this working together, we have had several projects already.

But now we want to enter also into dialogue, into sharing our views, our religions with one another. Therefore, we plan also to make use of the help of guest speakers. And so, you are the first guest speaker in the context of this programme of interreligious dialogue between the religions here in Suriname. We thank you for your preparedness to come and share your views with us. And the topic for this evening is 'The Shariah' or 'The Relation between Religion and Politics in Islam'. And that's against the background of the cooperation of various religions in one country.

And second item on the agenda is, the Ahmadiyya question. The deeper background of the persecution of the Ahmadiyya Muslims.

Once again we thank you for your coming here, and we hope that this evening will be for you, and for us all, a pleasant dialogue, a brotherly experience and also a fruitful experience for the benefit of a better relation between the various religions here in Suriname and in the world.

May I invite you now to address our community?

The Relationship between Religion & Politics in Islam

Speech by

Hazrat Mirza Tahir Ahmad, Khalifatul-Maish IV[rta]

After recitation of *tashahhud* and *ta'awwuz*, in Arabic, Hazrat Khalifatul-Masih IV[rta] said:

Your Lordship the Bishop, the General Secretary of this Association and all the distinguished guests, ladies and gentlemen:

It is indeed a signal honour for me to be invited this evening as the first guest speaker in the history of this Association. It is a historic moment for me, to share this experience with you of free, adult dialogue without excitement, without emotion, just to put our views across like normal human beings, in all decency, to make ourselves better understood by others, and to try to understand others better. That is the purpose of free dialogue, and I am so glad that you have undertaken this noble task, because the world today does need it very much in every sphere of life.

As far as the question on which I am desired to speak, I must apologise first of all, by pointing out that both these subjects are very vast, and perhaps in the limited time at our disposal, it will not be possible to do justice to even a single subject. So I propose that after I have finished on the first aspect, that is 'Shariah and Politics—the Law of Shariah and Imposition of Shariah Law in any Country', when I have finished speaking, if we find more time, then I would turn to the other subject; otherwise, we should like to leave it at that, because then it will give you opportunity to contribute your views, and to ask any questions if you so desire.

Anyway, I will try to be brief, but also one has to be comprehensive. The Shariah law is now a question which is very hotly debated among Muslim countries.

Enactment of Shariah Law in Pakistan

Recently, Pakistan has been the seat of this hot—sometimes violent—controversy about the Shariah. It is understood generally that if the majority of a country is constituted of Muslims, then the Muslims have a right—rather, an obligation—to enact Shariah law. It is argued that if they believe in the Holy Quran and if they believe also that the Holy Quran is a comprehensive Book which relates to every area of human activity and directs man as to how he should conduct himself in every sphere of life, then it is hypocrisy to remain contented with those claims. They should follow the logical conclusion and enact Shariah law and make it the only law valid for the country.

Now, this is what is being said on the one side. On the other side, many difficulties are pointed out such as proposed legislative problems—very serious constitutional problems—as well as very serious problems in almost all spheres of the enactment of Shariah. So, let me first briefly tell you why Shariah law cannot be exercised or imposed on a people, who practically, as far as their normal way of life is concerned, are not ideal Muslims, much to the contrary. In those areas where they are free to practice Islam, they fall so much short that one wonders: When they willingly cannot exercise Islam, how could they be expected to do it by coercion and by force of law? This and many others axe the areas when debate is being carried on and pursued hotly, but I'll now very briefly enumerate the points to make you understand all the sides of this issue.

Personally, I have also been participating in this debate which was going on in Pakistan and many a scholar, who came to London or who wrote to me for guidance, were helped by me. Though I did not entirely dictate notes to them but to a great degree they were helped by me to understand the problem in larger perspective. Thus, many an article that have been published in Pakistan did have my opinion also expressed in them.

Shariah is the law and there is no doubt about it; the law of Islam; the law for Muslims. But the question is how far this law can be transformed into legislation for running a political government. On top of that, many other issues get involved in it. For instance, if a Muslim country has a right to dictate its law to all its population, then, by the same reasoning and the same logic, every other country with the majority of its population belonging to other religions would have exactly the same right to enact their laws.

The entire world would become a world of not only political conflict but also of a politico-religious conflict, whereby all the laws would be attributed to God, yet they would contradict each other diametrically. There would be such a confusion that people would begin to lose faith in a God who speaks one thing to one people and another thing to another people, and who tells them to enforce this law on the people or 'they will be untrue to Me'.

As such, you can well imagine what would happen in India for instance, if the law of the Hindu majority is imposed on the Muslim minority. As a matter of fact, a large section of the Indian society is gradually being pushed towards this extremist demand by way of reaction—I suppose—to what is happening in some Islamic countries. What would happen to the Muslims and other minorities of India? Moreover, this is not a question of India alone. What if Israel enacts the law of Judaism—the law of the Talmud? I have read it and I know it will be impossible for any other non-Jew to live there normally and decently.

In the same manner, Christianity has its own rights and so has Buddhism.

Participation in Legislation

The next consideration is the very concept of the state. This is the most fundamental issue which has to be resolved and addressed by those who are concerned with politics or international law. The question is that anyone born in a state has a right to participate in its legislation.

In the secular concept of the running of governments and legislation, everyone born in a given country—whatever be his religion, colour, or creed—acquires the basic fundamental civic rights. And the most Important among these rights is the chance, at least, to participate in the shaping of legislation.

Of course, parties come and go; majority parties today may turn into minority parties tomorrow. Everybody's wish is not fulfilled or carried out, but, in principle, everybody has a fair chance and an equal chance to make his say heard—at least by the opposition—on matters of common principle. But what would happen if one Shariah or one religion is imposed as the law of that country? If Muslim law were imposed in a country, all the rest of the people, who are inhabitants of the same land, would have to be considered as second, third, or fourth rate citizens of the same country with no say whatsoever in the legislation. But that is not all, the problem is further complicated within Islam itself, because Islam has a Book revealed by God and the Muslim scholars claim that it is their right to interpret the Book.

Legislative Body Subordinate to Religious Scholars

On issues of differences of opinion, the legislative body stands subordinate to the scholastic opinion of such scholars who specialise in understanding the Holy Quran, or who claim to specialise in understanding the Holy Quran. What would be their mutual relationship? A body is elected to legislate. They legislate and you hear from some scholars of Islam that: 'What you have proposed as a law is against the fundamental principles of Islam. Islam has no room for such nonsense.'

Whose voice should be heard? On the one hand, it would apparently be God speaking behind those people, but only apparently. On the other hand, there will be the voice of a majority of people from the country. So the dilemma becomes almost impossible to be resolved.

All Religions Split into Sects over Time

But that is not all. Every religion, at the source, is one and single and inseparable, but as you pass along in period of time, the religion begins to diverge and split within and multiply, and become more and more in number, so that the same faith which, for instance, at the time of Jesus Christ[as] was one single Christianity, turned into many hundreds of Christianity.

Looked at from the vantage point of different sects, the one single source appears to be different in colour. Different coloured eyeglasses are used by various followers of different sects.

The same is true of Islam. It's not just a question of Sunni Islam and Shia Islam and how they interpret the Shariah. Within Shia Islam there are 34 sects whose interpretation of Shariah differs with each other. Again, within Sunni Islam there are at least 34 sects whose interpretation of Shariah differs with each other. There are issues on which no two ulemah of different sects agree—not just superficial issues—even the fundamental ones. You have only to read the Munir Inquiry [Commission] Report[1]. Justice Munir, the Chief Justice of the Supreme Court [of Pakistan], was one of the two judges appointed to investigate into the background reasons and the modus operandi of the anti-Ahmadiyya riots in 1953. Who was responsible and who was not?

How to Define a Muslim?

During the course of the inquiry, Justice Munir pointedly asked every Muslim scholar who appeared before him if he knew of a definition of Islam which could be acceptable by the other sects as well, which could equally apply to everyone and by the help of which we could define, 'Yes, this is Muslim', and 'That is not Muslim'. In the report Justice Munir submits that no two scholars of all the Muslim scholars interrogated, agreed on a single definition of what Islam was.

In the case of one particular scholar, he wanted some more time to think over it, and Justice Kayani who was a partner with Justice Munir, had a very peculiar sense of humour. His answer

---

1. *Report of the Court of Inquiry,* constituted under Punjab Act II of 1954 to enquire into the Punjab Disturbances of 1953. [Publisher]

was: 'I cannot give you more time, because you have already taken more than 1,300 years to ponder over this question. Is that not enough?

If thirteen centuries, plus some years are not enough for you to be able to define the very fundamentals of Islam—what is its definition—how much more time would you require?'

So this is a very grave issue. If the Shariah interpretation of one sect is imposed, then it will not just be the non-Muslims who will be dispossessed of the fundamental right of participation in the country's legislation, but within Islam also there would be many sects who would be deprived of this right.

The Interpretation of which Sect is to be Imposed on Shariah Law?

Again, there are so many other problems. For Instance, according to some, Shariah concept of punishment for a crime is so much different from the concept of another sect, that Islam would be practised in the world so differently on the same issue, that it would create a horrible impression on the non-Muslim world. What sort of faith is that which advises one punishment for the same crime here and another there? And in some other places it is just the very thing to do and it's no crime at all.

These and many such issues make the question of imposition of Shariah almost impossible. Moreover, the fundamental rights of other sects are also tampered with, or trampled upon, in many possible situations. For instance, on the question of drinking of alcohol; alcohol is forbidden in Islam, alright, but the very question of whether it is a punishable offence and whether the punishment, if any, is imposed by man in this world, is a fluid issue. It is a controversial issue and has not yet been agreed upon by all the people involved. What is the punishment for drinking? The Holy Quran does not mention any punishment. This is a fundamental law, the Book of law, and it is inferred from some tradition by some scholars that 'such and such' should be the punishment. But that inference is far-fetched and the traditions themselves are challenged by others not to be authentic.

So, will a large section of not only Muslim society, but also a large section of non-Muslim society, be punished for such reasons as in themselves are doubtful? Whether it is valid or not, this is the issue. Yet there are extremists everywhere and particularly those who go for Shariah to be imposed.

You will find many extremists who are totally intolerant of other people's opinion. Consequently, such grey areas will also be taken as *no doubt* areas by the extremists. They will say: 'Yes, we know; it's our opinion. It's the opinion supported by a medieval scholar of our thinking. And that is law.'

Difficulties Faced by the Pakistani Government for the Enactment of Shariah Law

Now this difference resulted in a debate in Pakistan very recently and Nawaz Sharif, the Prime Minister, had ultimately to decide that Shariah of no one sect will be adopted.

The law passed in Pakistan is that they will accept the supremacy of the Quran, and they will agree that no legislation will be made contrary to the fundamental Quranic teaching. But beyond that they will not adopt any rules and regulations which spring from laws as if they were legislative instructions from God. So, leaving that alone, what is left of Shariah is the general principle as enunciated in the Holy Quran, in the light of which an attempt would be made to Islamicise the country's laws.

So far so good. I think the Prime Minister has been able to extricate himself from a very difficult situation, but not for long. The ulema are already at his throat. Also, they are insisting that a Shariah Court should not only be continued—there is already a Shariah Court—to work, but its power should be enhanced. The final authority about whether the law is according to Islam or not should lodge with the Shariah Supreme Court.

As such, again, the power balance will be shifted from the elected members of the country to the extremist mullahs. So, once you accept something which is impractical to be imposed, then this will always lead to various troubles and it is impossible for you to carry on without further complications.

The Lifestyle of Today's Muslims is not Truly Islamic

That is one area of difficulties. But there is another very important area of difficulty; that is, the lifestyle of the Muslims in most countries is not truly and profoundly Muslim. You see, you do not require a law of Shariah to say your prayers five times. You do not require the law of Shariah to make you behave honestly. You do not require the law of Shariah to be imposed to make you speak the truth and to appear as witness in court—or wherever you appear as witness—honestly and truthfully.

A society where robbery has become the order of the day; where there is disorder, chaos, usurpation of others rights, where the courts seldom witness a person who is truthful, where filthy language is a commonplace mode of expression, where there is no decency left in human behaviour—what would you expect Shariah to do there? How would the law of Shariah genuinely be imposed in such a country? This is the question.

Suitable Atmosphere Required for the Imposition of Shariah Law

I have given a different form to this question and this was raised of course, and so far, I have not heard of any answer which really could resolve the issue.

The question is that every country has a climate and not all the flora can flourish in that climate. Dates flourish in deserts but not in the chilly north. Similarly, cherries cannot be sown in the desert; they require a special climate. Shariah also requires a special climate, if you have not created that climate, then Shariah cannot be imposed.

Every prophet—not only Prophet Muhammad[sa]—first created that healthy climate for the law of God to be imposed, willingly not compulsorily. And when the society was ready, then the laws were introduced and stiffened further and farther, until the whole code was revealed. That society was capable of carrying the burden of the law of religion, whether you call it 'Shariah law' or any other law.

In a society, for instance, where theft is commonplace, where telling falsehood is just an everyday practice, if you enact Shariah law and sever the hands of those who steal, what is going to happen? Is that the purpose of Shariah? It's not just a question of sentimentality about religion. God's will be done no doubt, but it will be done in the orderly way as God wishes us to do.

Shariah Law Used as a Pretext to Seize Power

I have suggested to certain political leaders that they should invite all the Muslim scholars to reform one small city of Pakistan first, and then have the Shariah imposed there. For Instance, Faisalabad is a small city—or a big town—of mainly traders, famous for its corrupt practices.

I proposed that the ulema should be invited from all over Pakistan to first reform the society of that single town. When the people of that town have become capable of carrying the burden of Shariah, then the government should be invited to come in and take over the administration of the law of Shariah.

But it will not happen. They don't care. They are not concerned. It is not the love of Islam which is urging them on to demand Shariah law. It is just an instrument to reach to power, to capture power and to rule the society in the name of God. Society is already ruled by corrupt people, by cruel people, but that is done in the name of human beings. That is tolerable to a degree, but when atrocities are committed in the name of God, it's the worst possible—the ugliest thing—that can happen to man.

So as such, we must think many, many times before we can even begin to ponder over the question whether anywhere in the world, the law of religion can be imposed as a legal tender.

Personally, I doubt it.

Now, that is where I rest the case for a while. If you think there is time to turn to the second question, then I will do so. Otherwise, we will sit and discuss this—what I have already said.

QUESTION & ANSWER SESSION

After the speech many questions were put to the speaker and below are the answers to some of them. Unfortunately, as will be noticed, some questions were not recorded properly, however the answers do indicate what the question was about.

QUESTION—There is a particular confusion in the Western world about Shariah...

ANSWER—Thank you for this pointed question. But I thought that such questions were outside the realm of discussion.

What we are discussing is whether it is possible to adopt religious law as the law of the country by any state, or any other religion for that matter.

I believe it is not possible. It is not possible even if you genuinely and fervently so desire; in the name of God, even then it's not possible. We have gone so far away from religion. We have become hypocrites. The whole human society has become hypocritical. There is hypocrisy in politics and society everywhere. And hypocrisy does not permit honesty to flourish. It does not permit the word of God to take root. That is the main problem.

QUESTION—I feel that we cannot really apply a law that came for older times to the modern times. Please explain.

ANSWER—I have studied this question in depth. I believe that religion can be permanent and universal provided its principles are deep-rooted in the human psyche. The human psyche is unchangeable.

And that is exactly what the Holy Quran claims. It says it is *deen-ul-fitrah,* meaning a faith or a law based on human nature. And also *laa tabdeela li khalqillah,* meaning that the creation of God and whatever He has created in you, the dispensation, the dispositions, etc. and the basic propensity to do something or not to do so, all these remain the same.

Consequently, any law which is rooted in human psyche, must also be universal and permanent. But, the Holy Quran does not stop there. It does not monopolise this truth. It goes on to say that all the religions, at their nascent stages and at the stages of their development, were fundamentally the same and they all carried such basic truths as were related to human nature. This is referred to by the Holy Quran as *deenul-qayyimah.* It says there are three fundamental features in every religious teaching:

Firstly, to mend your relations with God; to be honest and devoted to Him.

Secondly, to worship Him. In the Quranic sense, worship does not mean just to pay homage by lip service, but to try to acquire God's attributes.

And thirdly, to do service to mankind and spend in the cause of the needy.

These are the three fundamental branches, according to the Holy Quran, which are common to all religions. However, with the passage of the time and through interpolations they were changed later on. So, what is needed is rectification of the change, not a new faith. And that is what has been happening with the advent of every prophet.

So, it is a highly complex question and also not directly related to the issue we are discussing. I hope this much should suffice.

As far as the question of whether Islamic law, or any other religious law, can be imposed perforce, I say 'no' because it is against the spirit of religions themselves! The Holy Quran says:

$$\text{لَآ إِكْرَاهَ فِى الدِّيْنِ}^{1}$$

Laa Ikraaha fiddeen (al-Baqarah, 2:257)

This is a statement of the Holy Quran of course, but it is

---

1. There should be no compulsion in religion (*Surah al-Baqarah,* 2:257). [Publisher]

a universal statement which can never be changed. It is an example of how laws can become permanent and universal. It says there is no coercion in faith or in matters of faith. No coercion is possible and no coercion is permitted.

So, here is the question: If one religion imposes its law on a society where people of other religions and denominations also live, how will this verse stand against your attempt to coerce? Not only vis-à-vis the people from other religions, but vis-à-vis people from the same religion who are not willing.

So, this is the fundamental question. Therefore the conclusion is that coercion is not an instrument in religion, and certainly not a valid instrument in religion.

The only authority in Islam, which was genuinely capable of being given the right to coerce, was the founder of Islam, Prophet Muhammad[sa]. Why? Because he was a living model of Islam and because when enquired about his character, his holy wife, Hazrat Ayeshah, said he was the living Quran.

So, the only person who could be genuinely entrusted with the faith of others, and be permitted to use coercion also where he felt that rectification was to be made by force, was the Holy Prophet[sa]. Yet, addressing him, Allah says in the Holy Quran:

$$\text{اِنَّمَاۤ اَنْتَ مُذَكِّرٌ ۙ لَسْتَ عَلَيْهِمْ بِمُصَيْطِرٍ}[1]$$

---

1. For thou art but an admonisher; You are not a warden over them (*Surah al-Ghaashiyah*, 88:22–23). [Publisher]

Innamaa anta muzakkir lasta alaihim bi musaitir (*Surah al-Ghaashiyah*, 88:22–23)

You are just an admonisher. No more. You are given no authority to coerce. You are not a superintendent of police. *Muzakkir* is exactly the superintendent of police.

So, that is why I say neither coercion is possible, nor permitted by God. Moreover, what prevents a Muslim from following the Muslim law? Why should he wait for the whole legislation to be changed?

Most of Islam, Christianity and Hinduism can be practised without there being the law of the country. The more so since the general principle accepted by the modem political thinkers is that religion should not be permitted to interfere with politics and politics should not be permitted to interfere with religion.

Interference is what I am talking about, not cooperation. Cooperation is the second part of the same subject. So, if a society is permitted to live according to their own religious aspirations, why should the religious law concerned be made law of the land?

I quote an example of how the Shariah law has already failed in Pakistan. During the late General Zia's regime, Muslim Shariah Courts were also constituted. And the choice was left to the police either to charge a criminal and channel him through the Muslim Shariah Court or to channel him through the ordinary court. Do you know what the result was? Hardly any case was tried by the Muslim Shariah Court because the police had raised the price of bribery and they threatened everyone that if they did not pay double the price of the ordinary bribe, they would channel their case through the Shariah Court.

That was the net outcome. And you will be surprised to find that out of thousands and thousands of possible choices, hardly two or three were those which were directed through Shariah Court and also because of political pressure. Because some political parties wanted to punish their enemies and they wanted such cases to be tackled by the Shariah Court.

So this the reality of life. How can we change it?

QUESTION—So what is the reason for the change in laws as new prophets came along?

ANSWER—First of all let me say that this generalisation is rather too bold. Because when you study the history of religion, it is not the case that every prophet came to change the law of the previous prophet's revelation.

More often than not, prophets came to strengthen the law and rehabilitate the law, rather than to change it. For instance, if you study the history of Judaism, you'll be surprised to find that even up to Jesus Christ[as], no new laws were enacted or introduced. They were changed or abandoned by the people, and efforts were made by prophets to rehabilitate them, to make people practise and to interpret them again in light of the original.

So, the history of religion as revealed to us by the study

of major religions of the world, tells a completely different story. Turn to China, for instance. Tao came with a teaching. Not a jot of that teaching was changed by Confucius. It was exactly the same teaching which was reinforced and re-interpreted by the latter.

But I agree. The Holy Quran also, positively dictates that, sometimes, the laws are changed. However, the question is are they changed in fundamentals or superficially? And how are they changed? Whether they require further change or not, this is also a very important question and a genuine question for me to answer.

Now, I quote three examples from history, of change of law of nature, ending up in the final verdict of Islam.

In Judaism, because of a long history of oppression by Pharaohs of the Israelites, the latter had lost that human quality of courage and defiance even when they were in the right. To take their rightful revenge was something beyond their power and strength because they had been trampled upon for far too long. This is similar to what happens sometimes to the Kashmiris in India: those who were cruelly treated started saying after a while, 'All right, we forgive our powerful enemy, but not the weak enemy.'

So, when such distortions appear, then the law has only to be a temporary law to rectify the error done. And that is exactly what happened in regard to the Mosaic law of revenge: Tooth for a tooth, eye for eye. And it was emphasised so much, as if there was no room for pardon.

That law was practised for a long period. Then came Jesus Christ[as]. By that time, the Jews had forgotten the very name of forgiveness. You have only to read Shakespeare's *Shylock* to know what they had come to. And if Jesus Christ[as] had permitted them also to take revenge, people whose hearts were hardened would never have forgiven. They would have said, 'Revenge is also permissible; why not take revenge?' To appease their own anguish.

So, Jesus[as] took away from them the right of revenge, but that injunction could not be a permanent one.

These are the areas where, sometimes, superficial teachings are revealed, but only for certain periods and for times, for historical epochs and not permanently.

Then comes the Holy Quran, and the law regarding the matter mentioned In the Holy Quran is:

$$فَمَنْ عَفَا وَ اَصْلَحَ فَاَجْرُهُ عَلَى اللّٰهِ ^{1}$$

Fa man afaa Wa aslaha fa ajrohu alallah (Surah ash-Shuraa, 42:41)

'You have a right to take revenge'. The whole verse in fact says: 'You have a right to take revenge when you are wronged. But not beyond the measure to which you are wronged'. This is one principle.
Secondly, you can also forgive, but not unconditionally. You can only forgive if your forgiveness promotes reformation; if it promotes crime, then you cannot forgive.

Now, this is the Quranic version which stands on the

---

1. But whoso forgives and *his act* brings about reformation, his reward is with Allah (*Surah ash-Shuraa*, 42:41). [Publisher]

summit of the development of the same thought. And, I have been meeting some Bahai friends, some other scholars from various parts of the world—I have travelled a lot—and I always give the following problem to them: Please try to change this law according to the new dictates of time.

So far, I have not met a single person who could suggest any change in this final law.

So, if the laws are resilient, accommodating and are based on principles and are also rooted in human psyche, I do not think that they need to be changed. But again, this is a discussion outside the main discussion. So please, I hope that would suffice and we'll turn to other guests, for any other question they would like to ask.

QUESTION—Please explain the difference between 'Shariah' and 'deen'.

ANSWER—Thank you. You see, *deen* is a word applicable to any philosophy, any *ism,* anything which you adopt as a course of conduct. For Instance, according to some Muslim scholar's idolaters had no *deen* and they would be abhorred with the idea that they did have a *deen.* However, the Holy Quran, addressing them says:

$$\text{لَكُمْ دِينُكُمْ وَلِيَ دِينِ}\;^{1}$$

Lakum deenukum wa liya deen (Surah al-Kaafirun, 109:7)

---

1. For you your religion, and for me my religion (*Surah al-Kaafirun,* 109:7). [Publisher]

'You have your faith and I have mine'. When it is said:

لَاۤ إِكْرَاهَ فِى الدِّيۡنِ[1]

Laa ikraaha fid-deen (Surah al-Baqarah, 2:257)

The word *deen* encompasses every course which people adopt for their code of life. It is not just a faith in God. Even a denial of God could be a *deen*.

Shariah on other hand is founded on the concept of God. So, where a *deen* is founded on the belief that:

i. There is a God,
ii. Who also reveals His desires of how man should shape his destiny, and
iii. Where that will is defined in the form of certain laws or principles; that is called *Shariah*. Not necessarily that of Islam. Every faith has its own Shariah.

Now, the question is: Can Shariah be adopted even though it is not a part of the law of the land? We can quote an example from our Community that it is not impossible at all.

The fact is that almost every country of the world permits members of its society to resolve their differences mutually through arbitration. And in most countries, to my knowledge, arbitration is respected so much by the law

---

1. There should be no compulsion in religion (*Surah al-Baqarah*, 2:257). [Publisher]

that if irreversible arbitration is signed by both the parties involved, even then the Supreme Court would not annul that decision.

We have created a Qazaa Board and *qaazis* in the Ahmadiyya Community. And all Ahmadis who do not want to go to the common law for resolving their disputes and problems, they come to the Qazaa, signing a document that we, with volition and without any coercion, require you to resolve our dispute according to the law of the Quran.

And in such case, no government has ever interfered, no government has ever obstructed its passage and it goes on smoothly.

Similarly, as far as worship is concerned, it's an ongoing process that is carried on everywhere. Everybody is free to worship God as he pleases—or should be free—except Ahmadis in Pakistan, but that's a different issue. Otherwise, there is absolutely no attempt made by any law to obstruct the passage of worship.

Normally speaking, in most areas of life, Shariah can be practised without it becoming a law.

QUESTION—You have stated in your lecture, that the Prime Minister of Pakistan, Nawaz Sharif, has decided that the Shariah shall be the law in Pakistan without rules and regulations but referring to the Holy Quran. However, you find that this is not a practical way. I have observed that you have studied this subject very thoroughly. So, I want to ask your opinion regarding the type of legislation a country should adopt. Should the Shariah be rejected? Should it be modified? Should it be a secular type of legislation? What do you think should be the way out?

ANSWER—Thank you very much for this question, which I should have touched upon during my address. The fact is that the concept of government in Islam is a very important issue which must be resolved before we proceed further.

I have studied this issue in depth. I have studied the Muslim scholars of the past century who have spoken on this subject and written a lot on it, and who have not been able to resolve the issue properly. If Islam proposes a government which is representative of God, then the issue is to be looked at from a different angle altogether.

If, on the other hand, Islam proposes a system of government which is common to various denominations of religions and different people, then an entirely different outlook would appear.

In my opinion, the first is not the case because Islam pleads for the secular type of government more than any religion and more than any political system. Now, this is surprising for some, but I can quote from the Holy Quran and prove the point. The very essence of secularism is that absolute justice must be practised regardless of the differences of faith, religion, colour, creed and group. This, in essence, is the true definition of secularism, and this is exactly what the Holy Quran admonishes us to do in matters of state; how things should be done and how the state should be run. The Holy Quran says:

اِنَّ اللّٰهَ يَاْمُرُ بِالْعَدْلِ[1]

Innallaaha ya'muru bil-adl (Surah an-Nahl, 16:91)

'Allah orders you to always practise justice.' And then it develops the theme by saying:

وَلَا يَجْرِمَنَّكُمْ شَنَاٰنُ قَوْمٍ عَلٰٓى اَلَّا تَعْدِلُوْا اِعْدِلُوْا هُوَ اَقْرَبُ لِلتَّقْوٰى[2]

Wa laa yajrimannakum shana'aano qaw-min alaa allaa ta'dilu. I'dilu huwa aqrabu lit-taqwaa (Surah al-Maa'idah, 5:9)

'No amount of enmity between you and any other people should permit you to deviate from absolute justice. Be *always* just, that is nearer to righteousness.'

When you dispense your responsibility as a government, you must dispense those responsibilities with absolute justice in mind. Now, when absolute justice is established as the central theme of a government, how could Islamic law be imposed upon non-Muslims; because it would be against justice and so many contradictions would arise?

So, if you study this central core in depth, you will be surprised to find that the interpretation which I am giving to this, or that I understand to be the right interpretation,

---

1. Verily, Allah requires you to abide by justice (*Surah an-Nahl*, 16:91). [Publisher]

2. And let not a people's enmity incite you to act otherwise than with justice. Be *always* just, that is nearer to righteousness (*Surah al-Maa'idah*, 5:9). [Publisher]

is also the interpretation proved from the practice of the Holy Founder of Islam, peace and blessings of Allah be upon him. In Medina, when he moved there after Hijra, he came into contact with the Jewish and other communities who accepted him not as their religious leader, but a political leader. They agreed—and this is called the Charter of Medina—to refer to him all disputes and trust his superior judgment to resolve all the contentions between various parties. Islamic law had already been revealed at that time. Jews came to him for guidance or for decisions. Without fail, every time he enquired from them: 'Would you like your dispute to be settled according to the Jewish law or according to the Islamic law, or according to arbitration?'

Without fail, he never imposed Islamic law on a non-agreeing party, which did not belong to the faith. This is what I call absolute justice. So, absolute justice has to be employed by a truly Islamic government if it ever dreams of calling itself an 'Islamic government'. And this is in other terms, a secular government!

QUESTION—If you decide to have different legislation; legislation for the Hindus, the Christians and so on, I think it would be very disturbing in the society.

ANSWER—Exactly, that is what I am saying. I am not proposing that every political government should have a paraphernalia of legislation applicable to different religions. It's not possible. It's not practical.

CLOSING REMARKS

by the Chairperson

We are here working together, different religious communities—the Christians, the Hindus, the Muslims. It seems that we are working on a very good basis of mutual cooperation without interfering in the internal affairs of each other and on behalf of all organisations.

I thank you sincerely and I hope that when you will leave our country Suriname, you will leave it with good thoughts, good sentiments and also, leaving a lot of friends here.

I wish you a very safe journey.

PUBLISHER'S NOTE

References to the Holy Quran contain the name of the surah [i.e. chapter] followed by a chapter:verse citation, e.g., *Surah al-Jumuʻah*, 62:4, and counts *Bismillaahir-Rahmaanir-Raheem* ['In the name of Allah, the Gracious, the Merciful'] as the first verse in every chapter it appears.

The following abbreviations have been used; readers are urged to recite the full salutations when reading the book.

sa   *sallallaahu ʻalaihi wa sallam,* meaning 'peace and blessings of Allah be upon him', is written after the name of the Holy Prophet Muhammad[sa].

as   *ʻalaihis-salaam,* meaning 'peace be on him', is written after the names of Prophets other than the Holy Prophet Muhammad[sa].

ra *raziyallaahu 'anhu/'anhaa/'anhum,* meaning 'Allah be pleased with him/her/them', is written after the names of the Companions of the Holy Prophet Muhammad[sa] or of the Promised Messiah[as].

rta *rahmatullaah 'alaihi/'alaihaa/'alaihim,* meaning 'Allah shower His mercy upon him/her/them', is written after the names of those deceased pious Muslims who are not Companions of the Holy Prophet Muhammad[sa] or of the Promised Messiah[as].